Taking Time Out

Taking Time Out

Poems in Remembrance of Madness

THOMAS KRAMPF

salmonpoetry

Other Books by Thomas Krampf

Shadow Poems. Ischua Books 1997

Satori West. Ischua Books 1987

Subway Prayer and Other Poems Of The Inner City.
Morning Star Press, 1976

For Dr. Wm. Douglas Hitchings

Published in 2004 by
Salmon Publishing Ltd.,
Cliffs of Moher, County Clare, Ireland
Website: www.salmonpoetry.com
email: info@salmonpoetry.com

Copyright © Thomas Krampf, 2004

ISBN 1 903392 38 1

All rights reserved. No part of this publication may be reproduced or transmitted in any form or by any means, electronic or mechanical, including photography, recording, or any information storage or retrieval system, without permission in writing from the publisher. The book is sold subject to the condition that it shall not, by way of trade or otherwise, be lent, resold or otherwise circulated without the publisher's prior consent in any form of binding or cover other than that in which it is published and without a similar condition, including this condition, being imposed on the subsequent purchaser.

Cover artwork: *My Father's Madness*, Ceramic Sculpture by Gilda Oliver
Cover photography: Dirk Bakker
Cover design & typesetting: Siobhán Hutson

"Crime is a disease like any other malady...(therefore in a non-violent society) all crime including murder will be treated as a disease..."

GANDHI

Acknowledgments

Grateful acknowledgment goes to the editors of the following publications in which some of these poems have appeared:

Abiko Literary Quarterly, Baily's Beads, Home Planet News, New York Quarterly, Niagara Magazine, Phoenix Literary Quarterly Vol. III & IV, Poet's Theatre Anthology, Purchase Poetry Review, Earth's Daughters, The Buffalo News, Poets Against the War (online), and Today's Poets.

Contents

PART ONE – *Taking Time Out*

Taking Time Out	15
The Water Drum	16
St. Dymphna	17
Homage to Schizophrenia	18
Relocation	19
The Mosquito	20
The Glistening Rail	21
Aliki	22
Song of the Hunted	23
The Shawabtis	24
The Human Pyramid	27
Porquerolles	28
Window Poem	29

PART TWO – *Bestiality*

Bestiality	33
Meditation III	36
Golden Poetry Award	37
The Medulla	39
Snowplow	40
Mongolia	41
The Moonship	43
Montana	44
On The Shadowless Road	45
Partnering	46
A Short Canticle for Mary Magdalene	47
Hospice de Dieu	49
Death of a Flying Wallenda	50
The Demons	52

PART THREE – *Brain Disease*

Brain Disease	55
Judas	57
Shroud of Turin	58
Window of Opportunity	59
Wall Poem	60
Cinderella's Shoe	61
The Brown Hat	62
Rambo	63
The Black Canoe	65
Testament	66
The Crimson Petal	69
Slant Poem	70

PART FOUR – *Not An Apologia for Suicide*

Not An Apologia for Suicide	73
Alice	77
The Maggot	78
The Violin	79
The Ferris Wheel	82
Motionless	83
The Gingko Leaf	84
Elegy for Suicides	85
Among Hitler's First Chosen	86
The Euclids	87
The Bodhi Tree	88
Leah	89
The Man with the Black Nuclear Handbag	90
The Glass Slipper	93
Hell's Kitchen	94
The Birdbath	96
West Valley	97
Notes of a Voyage	98
Ground Cover	99
Notes	*101*

Part One

Taking Time Out

Taking Time Out

Do you remember
the madness of orange trees in Vence?

How over the dikes and valleys they hung
full ready to crash to the ground.

And before the long start of the fall, seeping up from the sea,
the miles of yellow mud split-level?

And then at noon, cultivated from the lips with no more than a yell,
the water came crashing through the poorly-constructed walls?

In the ground, the black fruit taking seed?

The Water Drum

I am inside the red vision.
I scrape down the oil tank with a wire brush.
The rust infiltrates my eyes, clothes.
It is now 15 years, since I jumped from the window, no almost 20...

Each time, I strike the side with the spine,
in a metal dust cloud, spirits appear on the hill.
They are neither Vietnamese nor Indian.
Nor wearing feathers.
But whether they wish me well, I don't know.

And each time, according to the level.
Smiling. The drumskin's beaded, tightened face.

The tone, the echo changes.

St. Dymphna

These stones have eyes. Dark, dark
as a shipwreck my skin.

They say leprechauns sprout from your fingers.
That's how wars begin.

Kilns fall flaming off the coast. My soul.
Around the white ash basin, I crawl.
I scrape my knees.

Those in your cells, drink from me.

Drink from me.

I am there.

Homage to Schizophrenia

Wearing a bridal veil
a charred and blackened corpse with no
head is pumping gas.

She has shorts on.

Once as a child, she stepped over an Indian.
He had his back turned to the sunset.
From the window, she watches the Hardly
Able Construction Company.

Suddenly, she elongates her eyes.

In the next room, as a woman steps from the water.
They are discussing a robbery.
Tattooed on her hip, she becomes a bird.

Mispronouncing her name, we call out in Aztec.

We are not yet able to confirm the angle of her flight.
Nor the color of her feathers.

Relocation

Driving home
past the house of my obsession
I see its emptiness
the moon a handicapped yellow
rising near the dikes
like a breath of bacteria
blown on the cheek
the empty space in the parking lot
the nameplate gone
from the window
without curtains

The Mosquito

When God kicked Lucifer out of Heaven,
he fell, splattering our windshield.

And later in the dark, when she thanked me for cleaning it.
And asked whose blood I thought it was.

I tried to tell her it was a mosquito's.

The Glistening Rail

My shadow attempted
suicide this morning

It attempted, like it did the other day, in the moonlight
to throw itself, headlong, under the wreck of a poem,
speeding down the tracks.

And like the 33,000, of all ages,
who succeed annually, in this country, and the 50,000
youths who make an attempt

And the 5 million survivors, in total
who are still living, but unspoken
for,

Had it not been for this poem
And the brakeman

It would have gone entirely unreported.

Aliki

Fucked-up
and wrapped-up
with her eyelashes
longer than her cigarette
she walks into the psychiatrist's
office
with its seagreen walls
and cubical puzzles
and portrait of a little French
village
he can escape to
in the summer where
Vincent Van Gogh
cut off his ear.

Song of the Hunted

It's snowing.

Now the hunters can follow the deer.
And walking toward him
barefooted

Before he goes mad
Nijinsky

His own bloody tracks.

The Shawabtis

Nemesis, so
often a goddess
lurching insane
and blue
in her chariot
with beak and claw...

hurtling, turns
so often
staring hatefully
in the dust
across the field
with mouth and eye
gaping startled
and burning
above the wheel...

gazing spitefully
toward them,
distant shadows
who so often
glazed in green
descend in couples
patiently to tend
the purple flowers
and hedgerows
of the dead

spirits, who
speechless like statues
with hoes
standing there
pale and inarticulate

sojourning among
the scarabs and vases,
so often dazed
a strange nourishment
cultivate for all
from the dark
and fertile embankments...

sleepwalking, perplexed
and triangular
with fingers of loam
in anguish down
through the centuries
compressed
against their sides,
perpetually figures
who released
so often rise from
palisades and chambers
and, like the living,
break the bondage
of the dead...

shadowy flames burst
watchful, cold
in eye and tendril
skirts of baked vine
which frozen spring
shimmering and divine
from the earth's broken
and galactic palaces,
a cat's paw yearning
heathen in stroke
and wistful laughter
for the health
of the burning sun...

while slow, Nemesis
around the dial
shrieking and chattering
so often speeds blue
like an hourglass
balancing a pyramid
upon her tongue;
a goddess enraged
and screaming scornfully
above the wheel,
staring at the yellow flowers
and thistles, gently
revolving before dawn
in the vast circumference
of the shadows.

The Human Pyramid

When inside myself

against the sun
the man at the bottom, missed his footing,
and from the wire, silently, masked,
they began to topple
like a cliff

I knew what was truly free,
might be possible.

Porquerolles

Juan les Pins
and the buoy floundering in the water
and the one you love
floundering in it
while you slowly
go mad
on the hot sand
if this happens and you still live you will be able
to walk with your head above the water
to Porquerolles.

Window Poem

I remember
once
I tore up a piece of writing
and threw it out the window
and shortly afterwards
I followed it
and now
I don't throw things out
the window
anymore
I hang on to them.

Part Two

Bestiality

Bestiality

In the bank.
I am changing accounts.
I'm going to have my own check.
With my name on it.
Establish my identity.
Be a man for the first time.
Not a poet.
Get things under control.
Financial.
She comes over.
I've been talking to Mrs. Brinkman.
The assistant vice-president.
She's been explaining to me credit.
Deductibility.
Percentages.
Monthly imbalances.
I make a joke.
Won't she lend me a million.
To start a worm farm.
She bends over.
She's been talking to Mrs. Brinkman.
Why can't things be as easy as that.
I see her breasts.
Mrs. Brinkman continues.
A monthly penalty.
Of course, if you get beneath a certain level.
Deposits.
Service charges.
The difference between five dollars and three.
You're losing money.
It makes no difference to me.
Contours.
Shadows.

She continues talking to her.
What is she saying.
I think of the farmer up the road.
Who can get the Playboy Channel.
On his satellite dish.
Like the marble eggs.
In his kitchen.
On the edge of a shelf.
Her breasts are so oval and perfect.
Of course, Mrs. Brinkman says.
There's always a risk.
She must know this.
The interest rates can go up or down.
Now she's trying to sell me the economy package.
16 checks at 25 cents each.
Or a five dollar monthly charge.
The woman stands up.
She arranges her blouse.
But with unlimited withdrawal.
They've finished their discussion.
She moves away.
I think of bestiality in Colonial times.
Or buggery as they called it.
Men making love with animals.
One man confessed to "having" five sheep.
Three goats and a calf.
Before they caught him.
And a turkey.
He had to line his whole flock up.
And identify his sexual partners
Before they hanged him.
But I can't tell her that.
She's picking a color for my checkbook.
I feel guilty.
They executed the sheep too.
"If it's a question of identity."

I almost start to say.
Or I could tell her about the half-man half-pig.
Born behind the Farnswell Cookie Factory.
I correct myself.
"I want the simplest possible thing."
I am also thinking of the man.
Who got caught in the near-by town of Cuba.
Sodomizing midget horses.
Expensive ones too.
Thoroughbreds.
But I couldn't tell her that either.
"Just a plain grey checkbook," I insist.
"With my name on it."
I look up.
Though it's not raining inside.
The other lady's coming down the steps.
Counting postage stamps.
Under an umbrella.
I look in my top pocket for mine.
Mrs. Brinkman has a knowing leer.
Almost a smile.
The guard too.
"But no phone number, please," I say.
"It's not necessary."

Meditation III

When he set her sandals
down, and holding her robe, turning
she stepped into them

I saw, riding tilted, a chariot
between the stars...

Before, I had only seen
emerging, once powerful, from the swollen
waters, an old man

...skin thrown over him like
loose burlap...

and a woman whose buttocks
were enormous...

Golden Poetry Award

"It's not easy to be a loser," I say.
To be disorganized.
Never get anything done.
To have your papers all around you.
Torn up & fluttering down.
Like when you jumped from the window.
"It's not easy to be confused," I say.
Even to write suicide notes which are awful.
Your last Will & Testament.
Can't spell, supposed to be literary.
Grammatically incorrect.
Wouldn't even win the Golden Poet's Award.
And everyone wins that.
Haven't met one yet,
"It's not easy, not easy.
To pick up a mouse-flower, headless.
In the morning," I say.
To spend all day writing about it.
And failing.
And never getting the bathtub cleaned.
Or the reviews done.
Or all the things you should have.
"No, it's not easy," I say.
"Not easy. To be disoriented.
A loser."
To suffer from Hypergraphia.
Like Arthur Inman.
His autobiography was 155 volumes.
And 7 million words.
Even I couldn't do that.
To have the muse picking flax from your sleeve.
And asking while the fat finger.
Touches the piano.

More lightly than it ever has.
If you're a poem inhabiting a body.
Or a body inhabiting a poem.
At least for now she's promised not to go.
And I believe her.
"No, it's not easy. Not easy at all.
To be disorganized. A loser.
A total loss."
Even my wife says it's hard to live with one.
I don't pick up my socks.
Of course she's only joking.
But then to be compassionate not only with others.
But toward yourself.
That's not easy either.

The Medulla

Tied down
Struggling, by the feet, the goat

In a pan
Catching his blood, as quickly we slice
Through his Adam's Apple

So from the first man
With a ripping of bone and cartilage
Rise words

Resurrected,
Like smoke, above Lake Titicaca

Snowplow

I lie in bed

A burning gate
a snowplow lights up the wall
it opens its wings

From my own depths
I cry out

Abba, Father.

Mongolia

This is my grandfather's stock.
This is my grandfather's race.
This is my father's forgotten history.
This is our ancestral tribe.

Down from the grasslands and fierce shepherds' huts
   of Mongolia
we come with wind-stretched pennants and whips of
   polished bone.
Up through the flat stomach muscles and bronze stretched
   ligaments
we ride with wooden stirrups and clenching teeth of
   crudely-filed gold.
Out of the blood's sleeping continental rivers like a
   haggard mist
we rise with frozen leather earstraps hung with tinkling
   silver bells.
Inside the brain's drifting grey countryside like speechless
   ghosts
we attack isolated peasant villages in hordes of shrieking
   infidels.

Westward from the horizon's closing mouth and smouldering
   cleft palate
we raise inflated sheepskin bladders and cruelly shake our
   rattles.
Northward through the disrupted marrow and fractured
   spinal vertebrae
we search for the spirit's deformed nerve roots beneath the
   mountain snow.
Eastward over the skin's dark forest blizzards and stupendous
   ravines
we imagine the distant clamor of our country's splendid
   halls and palaces.

Southward over the soaring cheekbone's gaunt and fluttering
 wingtips
we swallow chunks of rawhide while swiftly we goad our
 shortlegged horses.

Down from the grasslands and fierce shepherds' huts of
 Mongolia
we come with wind-stretched pennants and whips of
 polished bone.
Up through the ocean's sluggish loins and groaning
 seaweed memory
we hurtle across glands and lowland dikes... howling...
  like... a broken artery...

The Moonship

I awaken.
My drunken aunts.
We are driving in the graveyard.
Like the moon.
In a long white car.
Computerized, it's so modern.
The crawling beams.
Can't get the windows open.
Nobody can jump off.
Or out.
We pass my relatives.
Blow the horn.
Norbert's grave.
The angel's wings broken.
In an act of forgiving.
Like me.
Asking to be forgiven.
He tried to kill himself.
Tooting the light again.
We pass my grandparents.
My cousin Kevin in his mausoleum.
He drank himself to death.
My great grandparents.
My Aunt Connie.
"Let's fix her a stiff one."
Rowdy.
My 80 year old aunts.
In this moonship.
The only thing we have left.

Montana

Dave Smith.
I go to his room.
I have just talked to my Mom.
A dying woman.
"She's growing cold now," my sister Gioia says.
She places the phone against her ear.
"Mom," I say. "I'm far away. I can't come."
I love you. Let it go."
If only in answer to an inverted voice.
In an inverted phone.
The narrow constricted throat.
"Look," my sister says. "She's opening her eyes."
Now she's closed them again."
Dave Smith's a long time in coming.
I knock again.
Now I find out the reason for his delay.
I ask for a cigarette.
On a workbench under an open sky.
I am careful to take only one.
Dave Smith is pinning together Montana.
Turning when he was out there.
He has taken photos from every direction.
"Finally," he says, as I inhale. "I have it.
The missing pieces. The whole sky."
He is pinning it together.
I stare at ourselves in that vast reflection.
My Mother dying. The mining towns 25 miles away.
The mountains that can never be reached.
The spinners to be found in that bright debris.
The fishing tackle.
Only at high tide. To be lost again.
"Dave," I say, crushing my cigarette.
I avoid another. "Françoise says you're a lot like Jean.
You're both pure souls."
Now he's figuring out how to keep it all together.
"Aren't we all," he says.

On The Shadowless Road

Watching
you drive off to work
(you wave goodbye in
the rearview mirror)
I do too
nobody knows how lonely
I am under my hat
but I am not alone
under my hat

Partnering

Closure?
"Closure," she says.
"You have never seen her die.
Or your Father…
There will be no closure for you."
And what am I to say.
I sit and watch TV again.
The kicker loosening his leg.
Having missed 4 field goals.
He makes the fifth.
The ball hurtling end over end.
Over the wall forever.
"For you they'll always go on living," she says.
The tension in the stadium.
The ball blends into the dancer's thigh.
"And what if I could do that," I say.
"What if I could partner a poem like that."
Now partnering myself.
I become both the dancer and the dance.
Holding her and being held.
By the waist.
And the instep of the crotch.
As though she were glass.
With the weight of her flesh.
She has just rushed at me in full force.
I lift her.
Before setting her down.
And releasing her as I am released.
My hands are sure.
She knows as the poem knows.
She can trust me.
We both spin apart.
"You never finish anything," she says.
"I don't know how," I say.

A Short Canticle for Mary Magdalene

All her braids undone
her hair hangs down, past her waist
past her knees
"In this dark century," he says,
"dry your tears, Mary,
I am not your master, you are not my slave."

In this dark age, where shuffling papers
in vacant halls, her hair undone,
men walk up and down
he says, "Mary, restore your locks.
The bombs are falling.
Others are dying. Wipe not my feet for me."

If you like, shed them on the rich.
Or the shameful.
Shed them on those who kill the poor.
Or deny them.
Or for those who torture, in these dark times,
in vacant offices, while men walk up and down,
unbraid them.
"But shed them not for me, Mary.
Your hair's undone."

From the cities, wipe the ashes.
Embalm the dead, with your most precious ointment.
While in these dark days, men no longer
walk up and down,
with myrrh and frankincense, anoint the wounded,
the likes of which I never had.
"But don't, Mary. Don't cry for me.
Put your hair up."

Now past her waist
her hair hangs down, past her knees
all her braids undone
while out to sea, her Master's boat is gone
and in this dark land, men walk,
vacant men, shuffling papers,
these bright corridors.
And "You are not my master," she answers,
across the waters. "I am not your slave."

Hospice de Dieu

Referring to his injury,
like the Chinese women of old, she said, perhaps God
has bound your feet.

And dun-colored. He could only think of the wall.
If this were a state of grace. And why holding his skirts,
the angels of the Lord hadn't caught him.

Later, in binding the Chinese cabbages.
To make their hearts white and tender. At first, his
wife thought they might be for another.

He broke every one of them.

Death of a Flying Wallenda

In my necktie, businesslike though appearing, in my fall
There was sincerity.

The impact I wished to experience, naked.

And trying to sit when swept, from the rope by the wind, cleanly
It's how I spoke to God.

Don't be afraid, trembling.

Between the hotels, gliding verified a wire, down ten stories
Shattered, bone meeting patio.

It was ugly, true. And the blood.

For this I'm sorry.

And into emptiness stepping off, if in the beginning, wavering
Balance pole.

A human insect. To impress you, I ever sought.
Forgive me this also.

Such is God good

Nothing rooftops in San Juan, when I fell, nor in the bay
Warm winds, ships

Did I experience, if to console you

And plunging an accent

Fruitful, to your cold tropical gasp, such in his grace
Is he infinite

Never did I perceive them, the hotel windows

Or if so, I've already forgotten...

But why I had walked

Like the "flying men" by their teeth between Earth

And Heaven swinging around a pole

And of all creation first having asked permission

And The Tree itself

This time when I awoke I knew

Being neither drunk nor ecstatic...

They're still singing...in their loveliness

under the skies...

                the voices...

The Demons

Speaking to the
Demons, Christ the Great
Trickster said,
"Am I the Son of God?"

…In their illness,
affectionately, scratching
their balls, they said,
"Yes, but don't tell
anyone."

PART THREE

Brain Disease

Brain Disease

It's true.
My name is Jeffrey Dahmer.
And in cutting open my victims.
And as I dismembered them
Making love to them.
Like when I was being tutored,
As a youth in biology.
And as the prophet Nathan would say.
And the Psalmist in the Bible.
I took pleasure in the color.
And almost delectable variety.
Of their "inmost parts."
But this is not why after the first killing.
In a dark tunnel I continued.
Burying the body in a crawl space.
Even though I was afraid.
Afraid of that dark impulse.
But even more to turn myself in.
And a lifetime of madness.
But you will understand about the temple.
And to honor the bones.
Handcrafted in pewter.
The horseshoe crab in a necklace.
And their thighs hammered unevenly.
Among the skulls.
I once drilled while alive.
And filled with acid.
The frogs for silver earrings.
And what it might have been.
Had it been constructed.
(He was just a young boy.
I ruined a drill bit).
But under the Aztec Sky.

Sacrificed to the sun.
You will understand, won't you.
The face of my Father and Stepmother.
And those of my victims.
Before I ate them.
Reflected in the stone depression.
At the center of the wheel.
To catch the blood.
And the long surmounting steps.
Leading to all my possessions.
And the dark door.
Once I let someone go.
Because I was late to work.
(Even King David was conceived in sin).
And my need never to be alone without him.
Or the others.
Ever...

Judas

It wasn't perfidiousness.

It was a nightmare.

When alone under the garden's heavy tamarisk odor,
    at the gate,
you stepped forward to greet us,
and in the fresco's mulberry twilight, I puckered my lips,
I swear, I too, tasted around the rim of your mouth
the sweat turned to wine,
and inverted, with no handle, heard far inside of myself,
the faint ringing sound of a goblet.

I saw a sea of blackness wash back over
a tiny crystal of light.

It was then I knew I had to kill.

Or find somebody else to do it.

Shroud of Turin
for Pedro Medina

On Good Friday
a man, a convicted murderer
was executed in Florida.

Was he sufficiently dark?
Despite the Pope protesting
and another unexpected power
surge, they went ahead.

The man's black leather face
mask erupted in flame. The Vatican
commenting later said, "He was
burnt alive like a torch."

By now, the odor in Florida is as
familiar to us, as elsewhere.

At 3:00 P.M., the Governor entering
the Church, stopped. He vaguely remembered
the Shroud of Turin.

The frayed edges of the cloth.
How in the Cathedral bending over
he had imagined the eyes filled
with a strange light.

The faint odor of incense.

Turning to his entourage
he said to no one in particular
as a swallow flashed in the sun
as though on fire.

"Maybe we should consider changing
our method of execution."

Window of Opportunity

Unmedicated
the late March snow is swirling
madly over the hill

And as has been suggested
and we bear witness, in the museum of our memory,
behind the thick bull's eye glass

For those who go mad, on death row
or who are schizophrenic

If like the snowflakes
we can medicate them, in their illness
and briefly restore them to sanity

We can execute them
in their lucid intervals.

Wall Poem

Falange sky
and mud
sequence
and the blood of the angels
who cry
for their children
in doorways
who hold their eyes
in their hands.

Cinderella's Shoe

for Robert Brecheen

"It's not murder," I said softly
to myself, "but the law"

As ironically, and like Cinderella's shoe
and after taking an overdose, and being resuscitated
by the doctors working feverishly

Who declared it "mentally fit"

My own shadow arrived
just two hours late in its princely carriage
after the appointed hour of midnight

To lie down next to its own shadow
on the execution table.

The Brown Hat

They have taken my hat.
I know they did.
My brown hat.
The one that has no shape.
And that I got from Bolivia.
And wear in the garden.
Somebody came in the house.
And took the phone off the hook.
They were sitting there in my brown hat.
Making calls.
I know they did.
They left the receiver on the floor.
In the living room.
Who were they calling?
I hope it wasn't long-distance.
I know they did.
In New York you take the phone off the hook.
So the junkies can't call.
The line is busy.
Maybe they want to find out.
If they were really there.
I know they did.
Then they walked out.
In my brown hat.
The one I got from Bolivia.
And that's made from Alpaca wool.
And that I wear in the garden.
I know they did.
And that has no shape except for a tiny sun.
Rising in the hat band.
And that barely fits over my eyes.
I know.
I know they did.

Rambo

I go in the bank.
With my bag.
My blue denim bag.
My sack of poems.
I put it on the counter.
I search around in it.
The teller's eyes get big.
She thinks I have a gun.
To put her at ease.
I tell her of Rimbaud.
The French poet.
How he wrote his best poems.
Before he was 19.
I still have my hand in my bag.
Searching around.
Became a gun runner in Africa.
Carrying gold ingots.
Around his waist.
Never wrote a word afterwards.
In a season of drought.
I explain.
Like we're in now.
I see her eyes get bigger.
Hand move toward a hidden switch.
Stuck's her name.
Debbie Stuck.
I change my mind.
Better take my finger off the trigger.
Make a deposit quick.
Wavering.
I produce a poem.
My latest piece of writing.
I shift money around.

From one account to another.
I hold it before her eyes.
I'm no richer now.
No poorer.
She finds it beautiful.
She's relieved.
Checks my balance.
Gives me a deposit slip.
To go in my blue denim bag.
Next to the steel.
With all the others.
"I'll bet," I almost say.
I zipper it.
"A lot of strange people come in here."
But I don't.

The Black Canoe
for Anne Sexton

Blinded by the snow
she glides through the fields
in her black canoe
as the days get longer.

Testament

This is an audience performance poem. Anyone who wishes to join in at the chorus is cordially invited to do so. (It is important that the chorus be repeated after the poet). However, the audience should be warned this isn't a funny poem. It involves an old man, a WWI Army veteran, I once saw picking garbage in Brooklyn. For the purposes of the poem, "Oswego" should be pronounced "Osweego." Mr. Gunn was the man's actual name. Thomas Gunn. I have chosen to leave it that way.

(Are you ready?)

Mr. Gunn. He ate a piece of chicken. In Oswego.
Why, yes. He did.
Drumstick, flat as a steam iron, burning through water cress,
or asphalt, like a mule's kick,
or between anvil and hammer crushed, white meat separated from dark,
a knuckle's bare gristle,
toothless, he grins. he chews. he remembers it.
Why, yes. He does.

(Chorus): MR. GUNN. CHICKEN. OSWEGO

Of giblets dreaming. In gravy, he sits. On the stoop.
Why, yes. He does.
Gizzards, big as war. Amused, he thinks. He tilts his cap.
Bloody garbage trucks, plastic bags.
Guilty as onions, Eastward like crippled half-tracks or a pension check,
dripping they roar over the sun's greasy fretworks.
Dawn's fried liver, gullets. Chuckling hospitalized.
    He salutes them.
Laughing, he gnaws. He snaps the wishbone. No fingers.

Buzzards, wingtips burnt. On the mall. Does he remember
   them. Does he?
Pecking at an angel's bladder? Green marble? Fallen from
   the sky?
Like a mummy struggling? A garlic clove? With artificial limbs?
Why, yes. I'm sure. You want to bet?
I'm sure. HE DOES.

(Chorus): MR. GUNN. CHICKEN. OSWEGO

At 84. Garbage-picking. Healthy as a horseshoe. I watch him.
Yes, I do.
Box-bright. Empty. A present.
In Cuba. Or Normandy. Wrapping paper. With a sabre.
   Charges the hill.
AMERICA.
Off Atlantic Highlands. Minds cruddy. Surface the ill and aged.
Along the Gulf of Mexico. We stand guard. We shall attack them.
Technologically. We are sophisticated.
Against senility. The Big Dipper. Loping through the night.
We are Nazis. We shall use our radar.
Against helplessness. A Testament. Floating off Asbury Park.
Christmas lights. We shall drop our depth charges.
Against children. The Silent City. In pillboxes. Eyes hovering.
From our landing crafts. We shall storm the beachhead.
No doubt. Truthful. We are effective. We destroy everything.
Outside Keansburg. Mouth sagging. A dinosaur. On a ferris wheel.
Hunger. Rises from the ground.
Near Poughkeepsie. Greed. For warmth. In a Calypso. Huddled.
Over the water swings. A broken arm.
Between Twin Cities. A Dark Man. Always Masked. Spouting
   arrogance.
Toward the Super Bowl. Runs the Viking Gladiator.
In Seattle. Talcum on its testicles. Before a nervous breakdown.
Pride. Standing up. Hurtles on a roller coaster.

(Softly Chanted)

Up the river. In denial. Toward Skowhegan. Children's eyes.
Hopes. Lie clogged. Before the sawmill dam.
In the Legendary Midnight Hall. Near Akron. Painted by Picasso.
Fame's Stigma. A Card. Tumbles empty from a hand.

(A little louder)

Healthy as a horseshoe. Mindless, cruddy. At 84. I watch him.
Picking garbage. Ashamed. Both ways, he looks. He lifts the lid.
AMERICA. A widow's cry. In Appalachia or Gowanus.
   Emaciated.
Box-bright. Upside down. On the monkey bars. Ghostly
   hangs suspended.

(Moderato)

Aren't we going to change this?
Won't you please help us try?

(Pick one)

No, I won't.
Why, yes, I will.

(Chorus): CHICKEN. MR. GUNN. OSWEGO.

The Crimson Petal

A case of misperception...
The clock has distorted its hands...

And as the red rose is stalwart on the fence
we have implanted, in our desire to control
an electrode in its brain.

By searing memory...braising we call it...
we can create amnesia. Or a bit simplistic, the yearning
of the treated thorn, for the innocent bystander,
we can even teach it to kill...

        Or better yet
petals crisp in the evening frost, when returning home
from our walk, (they say if you've seen one injustice
you've seen them all)...

We can even make it redder against its will...

Slant Poem

I am the receptacle of the world
the wars of the century
a hypodermic needle away
take place beneath my skin
and the loves
and the ladies
in their gowns of crushed flowers;
I am the receptacle of the world
and so are you ...
with our punctured thighs
and our blood oozing out
back into the needle...

What are we to do?

Part Four

Not An Apologia for Suicide

Not An Apologia for Suicide

Like history, so clearly
bloody tongue
hacked off wrestling
at the root
and shrieking severed
by the wrist flung
into the dusty leaves
and bushes burning
under the sun
at the crossroads
of one's destiny

Blood-besmirched, leaves
like a cross
so freely in return given
and wrathful hung
around my neck…
undiluted, criminal why
do my fingers
like a silver leash
disoriented
across the ground
clanking crawl unchained…

Goblet shadows which so
wickedly pregnant
like a stench
staggering from cisterns
and the soul's dark cesspools
putrid spring rising…
while spirits malodorous
descend they also
down the temple's long steps
like snails
oozing in the sun…

Where eternally in hatred
stumbling back
from the rim of existence
voices returning curl
through the wall
enraged like the echo
of a madman's fingers;
and shadows, so ruthlessly
leaping, my own hands
from a millennium of plaster
toward my bed, darkly
racing come
to strangle me…

Around my throat, fingers
in their strength
so greedy and fibrous
like a cord
slowly and graciously
proceed to tighten themselves;
finally, among the shadows
lonely and ethereal
intent to kill
what mankind infinite
in his disgrace
has not yet succeeded
in killing…

While, in the moonlight,
dancing silver,
at the crossroads
and without malice
unmolested gather figures
with trembling lips
who, resolute and solid,
against the chalice

their own flesh rejected
gently place, and drink
from the golden cup
not their own
but of the world's blood
transformed...

Until, once again, shadows
like a grip
from around the throat
so strangely into the wall
at dawn receding
in a thousand shattered fingers;
proudly while, into the room,
like a ship
rising stricken from below
up the harbor
always floats calling
in the snow
the dark voice of hope...

Splits now my soul so gently
dark wide open
enormous like an icefield
or a seed
nudged by the burning prow
protruding from the wall...
and when not dispatched, hopefully,
by my own hand, I pray...
down, down turning cartwheels
and endlessly sinking miles
shall I tumble
past lodestones and rivers
black as glaciers;
finally, until one day, at long last
trembling and buffeted

by a greater hand of smoke
upward over the crackling treetops
and hideous canyon fires,
like a grey moth, or a kiss,
shall I also rise
wingtips outspread and membranes
trailing fire, scorched
but free, soaring
up the slothful cavern walls
from the furnace
toward the dark cold embrace
of the stars and universe
in friendship
gleaming just beyond.

Alice

Treetopping
Who fell
Alice who fell
In the arms
Of the Lord

Wrists severed
Who fell
Alice who fell
Treetopping
Into the arms
Of the Lord?

The Maggot

Down, I press.

Out it pops, the blow worm,
The skies,
By pus and blood, discolored.

"Love is ugly," I remember.

A nest, passing by the clouds,
Of this living flesh,
Before its consumption,

I reel, endlessly.

The Violin

I'm a violin.
Broken. In the streets. It slams down.
An engine hood.

Twisted, I walk. A bunch of strings.

"Hey, man?" He sits there, "Your legs?
What happened?"

"I jumped." In the shadows. Mysteriously.
I hold up four fingers.

"You're still alive, aren't you?" He stirs.
His friend. Now I see him.

"Thank God," I say. A chord. Nervously.
I search for it. Behind me.

"What'cha bust?" Around the wine bottle.
Golden. Floats a knuckle.

"What didn't I ?" The paper bag. I take it.
I don't even wipe the ring.

Up they leap, in the distance. The avenues.
Descending, a level.

Far off, rustling. Suddenly, I hear them.
I drink them, too.

Vibrating, into place. Water springs erect.
I turn the corner.

From the basin, a volume. Reach dark fingers.
They grasp the rainbow.

Across the channel's neck. Out of me, a hand.
Pegs tighten slender.

In the mist, anchored to a gap. The drawbridge.
Firmly closes.

Over the grill, flesh burnt black. She steps.
The dancer.

"Sangre Sagrada." Equatorial, she bounces him.
The sun, her child.

On a pedestal, madonnas in the window. Pigeons.
They hold them.

Before the Python God. Darkly chanting purple.
Slowly, they circle.

The rearview mirror, in the haze. Diminishing.
I adjust it.

"Look at his hands," I say. "They're like music."
We pass a bar.

Over the subways, crouching imaginary. He leans.
Eyes closed.

Palms fluttering, through the lights. The traffic.
He conducts it.

Deftly, he pulls. From the harbor's orchestration.
A ship's bassoon.

Tremulous, he directs. Painted tiny like a cart.
A mountain aria.

Darting, across the sky's embankment. The fibers.
Strokes a gleaming jet.

In a concerto, over my body's trestle. Slender.
Arching trails exhaust.

Drainage, polished wooden. From canals, my voice.
Upward floating skids.

Moonlight hollow withdrawn. To the storm, I offer.
A Rising Curvature.

The Ferris Wheel

Curtis
lost in your illness out there
among the moon and the stars
or perhaps stolen from us
by your own hand, I hope
out there among the galaxies
turning bravely on themselves
in slow fires…
like the ferris wheel
you once photographed…
that you are less lonely now.

Motionless

The fans remain still.
It's Good Friday. I go into the Church. I don't believe.
Anthony Barbaro. I cannot help thinking of him.
How some years ago. A student, a child.
He shot six people. From a high school window.
And overhead, in this Church. They seem to turn slowly.
Where he was an altar boy. With his corpse attached.
A member of the rifle club. He was a mere sixteen or so.
And how the psychiatrist. Declared him well enough for trial.
And just before. His room was also full of guns.
In shame and confusion. Only he comprehended how ill he was.
In his cell. The others spat on him. He hung himself.
And so, if I remember. In St. Mary of the Angels.
Each year, to pray for him. And for his family and the victims.
And the other wounded. I must believe in something.
Even if only the grey-hooded figures. Plastered in their niches.
Or the fans. Which are motionless.

The Gingko Leaf

Fragments.
I walk on the road.
Everything is to be perceived.
And not to be perceived.
The unborn.
Those who have gone.
Reddening the sky.
The sun comes up through the branches.
I walk.
Everything in my shoe.
My toes bent over.
To be perceived or not to be.
The shadow of the cats on the road.
Keeping pace with mine.
Everything is to be seen.
And not to be seen.
The goat limping in the morning.
Dawn wedged like a shelf.
Between the cloven hoof.
That can hurt.
It needs to be trimmed.
Everything is to be felt.
And not to be felt.
The metaphor.
Which we have learned to handle so carefully.
The Yellow Gingko leaf.
From ancient China.
Which fell so slowly over the centuries.
Into my poem this morning.
And now into yours.

Elegy for Suicides

As it listens

in an act of grief to its
own voice inside itself

my shadow clinging to the rocks
climbs down to the edge
of the sea

and commits to the waves
as it did for the twin
of its own shadow

the ashes of the Mother of Light
who killed herself.

Among Hitler's First Chosen

The grey cat is purring
like the sound of Zyklon B gas
getting ready to spit
from the gas nozzles.

And as mentally ill,
I lie in the bed, and chosen
among the first to go
I continue to stroke him

I feel his fur
grow cold on the inside
like the walls
of a crematorium.

The Euclids

I was mugged by my favorite hickory cane.
It was down by the projected Gowanus Swimming Pool.
I fell to my knees with a gaping hole ripped in the red-dirt
earth and torn wire fence of my imagination.
Unconsciously I put my hand to my nose but I didn't bleed.
I wondered as I slumped to the sidewalk who'd done all
    this to me.
I looked through the Spring leaves at a bemedaled factory chute
heavily armed and attacking ferociously across a roof.
I noticed drifting accomplished beneath the distant blue sky
the white project buildings suspiciously surrendering their eyes.
Somewhere I heard bulldozers crashing blindly through
    apple trees
and recharging with lowered blades into the root-stained loam.
Now I remembered counting earthdiggers on my fingertips
    in the sun.
Savagely they encircled me while I stood petrified and alone.
It is then I should have spoken within that snarling ring of fire
and asked myself what else I might have done.
Now I could hear the long green Euclids screaming still.
They were building a parkway through my shattered skull.

The Bodhi Tree

Under
the Bodhi Tree
the Bodhi
lies
green and flagrant
ecstatic in its wisdom
telling lies
and vulgar sonnets
that no truly lascivious man
dare speak.

Leah

My friend said in Rhode Island
when he was young, and his Uncle slaughtered goats
in their eyes, he could see the planes
leaving the coast for war.

And the other day
when we went to the barn, and I thought (she being old)
I was being merciful, and the one bullet John
another friend had, didn't work, (that was careless)
and he had to batter her skull

And she cried
in her illness, it would have been better to lie
down next to her and wait...

He said their eyes had a funny slant...

I could see the same dark planes taking off
over the Atlantic.

The Man with the Black Nuclear Handbag

I am the man with the black, nuclear handbag.

Snowless, thighs burnt white as plutonium, outside the
 shopping center,
I watch the girl climb into the pick-up truck.

Just married, I think. I stare at the mountains.

Long-haired, perched on the seat, without the least sign of radiation,
or even an explosion, she drives off.

Muttering, I leave the broken hobby horses. I follow the President.
He and I, we like the music. Sometimes, we go inside.

A girl, behind the counter, she watches my handbag. Black, nuclear.
Smiling, I watch her eyes. She's friendly.

She knows. The President and I, we could destroy everything.

Does he remember? I ask myself. Does he?

Up the aisle. By the stationery department. Under the lights,
we turn. They gasp. We're happy.

All eyes follow us.

Once in the City, we entered a brake repair shop. Together.
The President, not I, excused himself.

Politely.

I was left alone, surrounded by old carburetors. All alone.
The President, not I, he had to go to the toilet.

What's that? asked a mechanic. Greasy, he looked up from an engine.
He pointed at my handbag. Nuclear, black.

With a wrench.

Nothing, I stammered. I was upset. *Why didn't he work on brakes?*
Top-secretly, I tried to smile.

Looks like somethin' an old lady would carry, he added, snarling.
He was banging on a generator.

Relieved, I heard the President. He had pulled the toilet chain.
Quickly, I recovered.

From the ceiling fixture, water roared down.

Pretty old-fashioned, I muttered. I felt a surge of confidence.

Somebody get me a paper towel? asked the President. He stood there.
He was annoyed. I can always tell.

At the cash register, others step aside. We protest.
It's like that.

The President and I, we always buy fuses for the White House.
Together.

We laugh. The girl returns our change. Fumbling nervously.
Together, we crack a joke.

We always try to put people at ease.

Outside, I see the same girl. The President, he grabs my arm.
I stare at the mountains.

Thighs white as plutonium, she descends from the pick-up truck.
Just married, I think. She's forgotten something.

The President, he's hurting me. He's shaking me, violently.
I look at him. He's frightened.

THE CODE, he's shouting. WE'VE BEEN ATTACKED.

Everything's silent. I'm glad. I can't stand shouting.
Quickly, I open my handbag.

Black, nuclear.

The President, he was hurting my eardrums.
I think of all my friends.

At work, in other countries. Like me.
The President laughs.

Madly, I smile.
I hold up a rose.

The Glass Slipper

Only the soul can walk in glass slippers.
Only the soul can slip its toe into the blown glass
shaped like a bottle.
Only the soul can walk up and down on the earth
like lovers.
Only the soul can know death and live.
Only the soul can resist the bulldozer's teeth
and the journey between kingdoms.
Only the soul has a glass buckle which is chipped.
Only the soul doesn't ask why the poet has buried
the slipper with his fantasy.
Only the soul knows the lover can give no answer.

Hell's Kitchen

Pointing upward
my grandson asks me where
Heaven is.

I start to say, it doesn't exist.
It is a thing of our imagination.

But then I think
she being French, perhaps it is like the back porch,
or Françoise's kitchen.

She says wherever the kitchen is.
That is actually the front of the house.

So the back porch is the front.

That is very important for the French.
And the front the back.

And whenever we think we are entering.
Or coming up the driveway.

While driving down.
It is a good thing he doesn't ask where Hell is.
He stirs on the couch.

Or is he just about to?
We are exiting.

But quickly I think, as we watch TV.
And kitchen or no kitchen.
I remember a poem.

And a player is writhing on the ground.

Heaven is when you are close to God.
This seems to satisfy him.

And Hell is being far away...

The Birdbath

If all the religions of the world
came to worship on my front lawn
I think (provided the grass were cut)
God would be pleased...
The Jains walking around *ganz
naked*, with a cloth over their mouths
so they wouldn't hurt the air...
the Catholics in their robes wishing like
the Moslems, they could have colorful
underwear, or like the ancient
Hebrews, praising the psalms, bang
castanets or play cymbals, or even like the
Indians (Native Americans, that is), in
praise of water, picking up the sunlight, and
letting it flow through their fingers, yes,
if all the religions of the world came
to pray on my front lawn, I think God would be
very happy, the song, the dance, the colorful
robes, the bartering voices, the variety, and
even over by the birdbath, that single
atheist feeding the birds, I think God would
be especially happy with him, even if the
lawn weren't cut...

West Valley
After Orozco's Dartmouth Murals

stepping down even from the image of his own crucifixion
and like a car compactor in a junkyard
the instruments of war
crushing beneath his gaze...
Christ broke the timbers   across his back

Notes of a Voyage

I have been to London
Dublin, Paris

Seen when the Queen is in
her entrance, in Buckingham, beneath
the raised incisors of a gate
in her stately carriage

In Westminster, the corroded iron
of Chaucer's tomb, and next to it,
unpretentious, John Clare's

                opening on a open field
                of madness

But here underfoot
I have all I need, a snake fleeing
bright as razorwire
in the grass…

Ground Cover

Drawing blood
my illness intensifies itself
a hybrid in the sun

It is when left alone
to surrender in the darkness
its briars

It becomes, blossoming
above the rocks, below
them beyond

the gentlest flower
in my garden

Notes

PAGE 15… "Taking Time Out." The Mediterranean town of Vence is situated on the Cote d'Azur in France about 15 miles inland from Nice.

PAGE 16… "The Water Drum." The poet was younger when he wrote this poem.

PAGE 17… "St. Dymphna." Born in Ireland, St. Dymphna is patron saint of the mad. As a young woman, she fled to Belgium where she was eventually murdered by her Father, who had pursued her. The site where she died, Gheel, is still known today for its miraculous healings of the mentally ill.

PAGE 23… "Song of the Hunted." Nijinsky is the famous Russian ballet star who went mad and who died after being institutionalized for years. His diary is a painful but important record of his descent into illness.

PAGE 24… "The Shawabtis" are tiny statues or figurines the Egyptian bury with the dead to carry on tasks in the afterlife.

PAGE 28… "Porquerolles" is a Mediterranean island near Toulon in France.

PAGE 33… "Bestiality." The 'Cuba' mentioned in this poem is a small town near the poet's home in Western New York

PAGE 49… "Hospice de Dieu. 'The Hospice of God' was an old military-civilian hospital in Aix-en-Provence, France. The 'angels of the Lord' catching one up is a reference from both the Old and New Testaments.

PAGE 55… "Brain Disease." Jeffrey Dahmer is one of a number of serial killers who has come to prominence today. This is a poetic interpretation of a diseased mind.

Page 59... "Window of Opportunity." Concerning capital punishment, it's still an open question in the U. S. as to whether one can legally medicate the mentally ill to make them sane enough to execute.

Page 73... "Not An Apologia for Suicide." This is a description of an actual suicidal state when one's mind and psyche has turned against oneself. It is as personally accurate as one can make it. The poem also has within it a crucial moment when both survival and redemption become possible.

Page 87... The "Euclids" are earth digging machines.

Page 88... "The Bodhi Tree." This is the tree Buddha sat under when he got enlightened.

Page 90... "The Man with the Black Nuclear Handbag." In each country that has nuclear weapons there is a man following the president or leader with a briefcase containing the nuclear codes. This is in case of a surprise attack.

Page 98... "Notes of a Voyage." John Clare is a 19th Century English poet who went insane. He is commemorated in the Poet's Corner in Westminster Abbey.

About the Author

Thomas Krampf is the author of three prior books of poetry, *Subway Prayer and Other Poems of the Inner City*; *Satori West*, and *Shadow Poems*. He has read in universities and on the media. For many years, he specialized in teaching poetry and creative writing to learning disabled adults and children. He has also taught in drug rehabilitation centers and prisons. He now lives in western New York State with his wife, Françoise. They have three daughters and numerous grandchildren.